Depression is a mental health disorder characterised by **persistent feelings of sadness,** hopelessness, and a loss of interest or pleasure in activities. It goes beyond normal fluctuations in mood and can significantly **impact a person's daily functioning,** relationships, and overall quality of life.

While everyone may experience temporary feelings of sadness or low mood, depression is **more severe and long-lasting.** It can affect people of all ages and backgrounds, and it is **not a sign of weakness or personal failing.**

If you or someone you know is experiencing symptoms of depression, it's crucial to **seek professional help.** Treatment options for depression may include therapy, medication, lifestyle changes, support groups, and self-care practices.

Remember, **there is hope and support available** for those affected by depression. With the right treatment and support network, individuals can find relief and regain a sense of well-being. It's important to prioritise mental health, seek help when needed, and remember that **you are not alone in your journey.**

CREATE A BRIGHTER FUTURE

You are not defined by your struggles, but by your
incredible spirit and the determination to create
a brighter future. Keep talking, keep reaching out,
and know that I'm here for you,
every step of the way.

Hey, I get it. Depression can feel like
you're stuck in a never-ending loop
of gloom and doom.

But trust me, there's a light at the end of the
tunnel, and I'm hoping you find it one day.

Remember, storms may rage and waves may crash, but you are the captain of your own ship.

Steer yourself towards calmer waters, adjust your sails, and navigate through the tempests with unwavering strength.

CREATE A BRIGHTER FUTURE

It's okay to not be okay.

You can vent, cry, or even crack a joke
if that helps lighten the load.

Imagine a garden blooming with resilience.
Each day, tend to your own garden with self-care,
nourishing it with patience, kindness,
and compassion.

Watch as the seeds of healing take root and
blossom into a life filled with purpose and joy.

CREATE A BRIGHTER FUTURE 

Some days feel like a heavy rainstorm,
but remember, even the darkest clouds
eventually pass, and the sun shines once again.

I know it's tough to see through the fog of
depression, but remember that there
are brighter days waiting for you.

I'll be here to remind you of your strength
and you will find the courage to keep going.

You are not defined by your depression. You are a beautiful, complex, and multifaceted individual with so much to offer the world.

One day, you will rediscover your worth and just embrace how the incredible person you are.

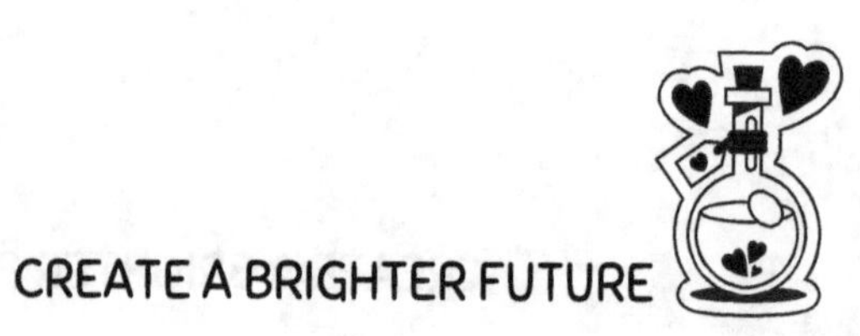

Depression can be like a heavy weight dragging you down, but trust me, you're stronger than you think.

Together, we'll find ways to lift that weight and let your spirit soar.

Sometimes, healing begins by acknowledging the cracks within us. Instead of hiding them, fill them with self-compassion, self-love, and acceptance.

It is through these cracks that the light of resilience and growth can shine through.

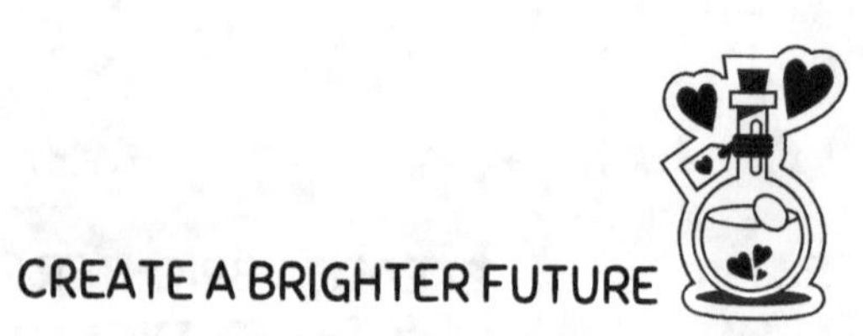

I want you to know that it's okay to ask for help. Seeking support doesn't make you weak.

It shows courage and a commitment to your well-being. Let's find the right path for you.

CREATE A BRIGHTER FUTURE

THE FLAME OF SELF-LOVE

You are deserving of love, care, and appreciation. Embrace yourself with kindness and compassion, for you are a unique and valuable individual. Cherish who you are and nurture the flame of self-love within you. You are truly worth it.

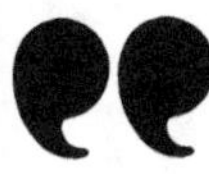

Take a moment each day to look in the mirror and say, "I love you" to yourself.

It may feel awkward at first, but over time, this simple act of self-affirmation can cultivate a deep sense of love and acceptance for yourself.

THE FLAME OF SELF – LOVE 

Self-love is not selfish; it's essential.

Treat yourself with kindness, respect, and compassion, just as you would treat a dear friend. You are worthy of your own love and care.

THE FLAME OF SELF – LOVE

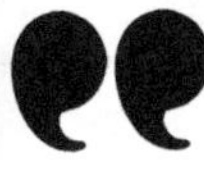

Believe me, you are a work of art,
a masterpiece in progress.

Embrace the journey of self-discovery and
self-acceptance, knowing that you are constantly
evolving into the best version of yourself.

THE FLAME OF SELF – LOVE 

Remember that self-love is
a journey of discovery and growth.

As you cherish and love yourself, you will uncover
new depths of strength, resilience, and inner
beauty. Embrace the process and celebrate the
remarkable person you are becoming.

THE FLAME OF SELF – LOVE 

Celebrate your accomplishments, big and small.
Each step forward is a testament to your strength
and resilience.

Be proud of how far you've come and excited
about the amazing things that lie ahead.

THE FLAME OF SELF – LOVE 

Take the time to nourish
your mind, body, and soul.

Prioritize self-care activities that bring you joy,
whether it's indulging in a bubble bath,
going for a walk in nature, or simply curling up
with a good book. You deserve it.

THE FLAME OF SELF – LOVE 

Take a moment each day to appreciate yourself.

Write down three things you love about yourself
or reflect on your accomplishments.

This simple act of self-appreciation can boost
your self-esteem and foster a deeper
sense of self-love.

THE FLAME OF SELF – LOVE 

Remember, you are enough, exactly as you are. You are deserving of love, acceptance, and happiness, simply because you exist.

THE FLAME OF SELF – LOVE

Practice self-compassion,
especially during difficult times.

Treat yourself with gentleness and understanding,
knowing that it's okay to make mistakes and
experience setbacks.

You are doing the best you can,
and that's more than enough.

THE FLAME OF SELF – LOVE 

Embrace your flaws and see them as
part of your unique beauty.

Remember that perfection is an illusion, and
it's our imperfections that make us human and
relatable. Love every aspect of who you are,
including the rough edges.

THE FLAME OF SELF – LOVE 

Dear, self-love is a lifelong journey, and it's okay to have ups and downs along the way.

Be patient and kind to yourself as you navigate through the process. Every step you take towards self-love is a step towards a happier and more fulfilling life.

THE FLAME OF SELF – LOVE 

Take time to honour your needs
and prioritize self-care.

Listen to your body, mind, and soul, and give
yourself permission to rest, recharge, and engage
in activities that bring you joy and nourishment.
You deserve to be taken care of.

THE FLAME OF SELF – LOVE 

Practice forgiveness towards yourself. Let go of past mistakes, regrets, and self-judgment.

Embrace the opportunity for growth and learning, knowing that you are deserving of forgiveness and a fresh start.

THE FLAME OF SELF – LOVE 

Again, self-love is a continuous practice, and it requires patience, consistency, and dedication.

Be gentle with yourself on this journey, celebrating each step forward and offering yourself compassion during moments of struggle.

A SHINING STAR

Hey, friend, you're a shining star in a galaxy of infinite possibilities. Don't let depression dim your sparkle. Keep being your awesome self, keep embracing the humour in everyday situations, and keep fighting for the happiness you deserve. The world is a better place with you in it.

Listen, depression might be like that annoying
mosquito buzzing around, but together,
we're going to swat it away.

I've seen your strength, and let me tell you,
it's inspiring. You've got the resilience
of a superhero!

You know, life is a bit like a roller coaster ride—full
of ups, downs, and unexpected loops.

But hey, even on the wildest roller coasters,
we always manage to come out laughing
and screaming for more, right?
So, don't sweat the dips. You've got this!

A SHINING STAR 

I have a feeling the future has some pretty
awesome things in store for you.

Just imagine, the world is like a big piñata, and
you're about to swing that bat of yours and
unleash a cascade of colorfull, joyful moments.
Keep swinging, my friend!

A SHINING STAR 

You're not alone in this battle, my friend. I'm right here beside you, armed with jokes, funny faces, and a listening ear.

We'll laugh, we'll cry, and we'll keep pushing forward. Together, we'll create a force field of positivity that depression won't stand a chance against.

A SHINING STAR 

Remember, my hilarious companion, laughter is your secret weapon. It's like a trusty sidekick, ready to leap into action and bring a smile to your face.

So, keep finding those moments that make you chuckle and hold onto them like treasures.

A SHINING STAR

Depression may try to cast a shadow, but I have no doubt that you'll rise above it like a shooting star.

You're a survivor, my friend, and nothing can extinguish your inner fire. So, keep fighting, keep laughing, and keep believing in yourself. You've got this, and I'm right here cheering you on.

A SHINING STAR 

One step at a time, one laughter-filled moment at a time, we're going to conquer this thing called depression.

I believe in you, and I know that brighter days are just around the corner. So, let's stick together, keep our heads held high, and continue this hilarious journey of life.

A SHINING STAR

You know, life is a lot like a chat with
a good friend – filled with moments of laughter,
heartfelt exchanges, and unexpected detours.

So, when things get a little shaky, don't worry.
when you encounter a bump in the road,
don't fret.

Lean on the wisdom and support of your
companions. Together, we'll continue this
wonderful conversation, embracing the
ebb and flow of life with open hearts.

A SHINING STAR 

Hey, my friend, I just want to say you're doing an amazing job navigating through this journey.

Seriously, you're rocking it like a boss! I know depression may try to bring you down, but don't you worry, we're going to give it a run for its money.

A SHINING STAR 

Let's make a pact, shall we? Promise me that you won't let those dark clouds dampen your spirit.

Promise me that you'll keep shining that light of yours, even on the gloomiest days. And promise me that you'll never, ever forget how incredibly amazing you are.

A SHINING STAR 

JOY IN THE LITTLE THINGS

Hey, my wonderfull friend, humour can be a powerful tool to lift your spirits and navigate through tough times. Keep laughing, find joy in the little things, and know that you have the strength to overcome anything with a smile on your face.

Let's face it, adulting can be overwhelming.

But hey, we can navigate through the responsibilities with a sprinkle of humour and the knowledge that we're all just making it up as we go along.

JOY IN THE LITTLE THINGS

You know, life is like a recipe with unexpected ingredients. Sometimes you get the sweet stuff, and other times it's a dash of spicy.

Embrace the flavours, my friend, and savor the culinary adventure.

JOY IN THE LITTLE THINGS

Life can sometimes feel like a never–ending
battle with alarm clocks.

But remember, you have the power to conquer
mornings with a cup of coffee and
a killer sense of humour.

You know, life is like a puzzle
with missing pieces.

Sometimes it's frustrating, but hey,
that just means we get to improvise and
create our own unique masterpiece.
Embrace the beauty of the imperfect.

JOY IN THE LITTLE THINGS 

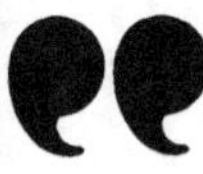

They say the early bird catches the worm,
but honestly, who wants worms?

Sleep in a bit and catch the late brunch instead.
Life is too short to miss out on pancakes
and extra hours of beauty sleep!

JOY IN THE LITTLE THINGS

Life can sometimes feel like
a never-ending game of "Whack-a-Mole."

But hey, let's grab that mallet of humour and
whack those moles of stress and worry away!

JOY IN THE LITTLE THINGS

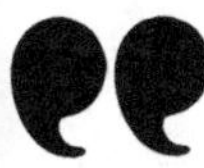

You know that feeling when you find a pair of matching socks in the laundry?

It's like winning the lottery! Celebrate those small victories and let them remind you that life can surprise you with little moments of joy.

JOY IN THE LITTLE THINGS

Remember, a day without laughter is
like a sandwich without the filling.

So, let's pile on the humour, add some extra
cheese, and make life a deliciously funny feast.

You know, life is like a giant game of
"Would You Rather."

So, let's embrace the absurdity and tackle each
question with a dose of humour and
a sprinkle of silliness.

JOY IN THE LITTLE THINGS

Let's be honest, nobody really knows
what they're doing.

We're all just pretending to be grown-ups,
stumbling through life, and hoping nobody
notices. Embrace the humour in
our collective cluelessness.

JOY IN THE LITTLE THINGS 

Life can be a maze, but let's navigate it with
laughter as our compass.

With every giggle, we'll find our way
to joy and happiness.

JOY IN THE LITTLE THINGS

LIFE IS A JOURNEY

Remember, my friend, life is a journey, and we're all navigating our way through it. Sometimes the path seems daunting, but with courage, self-compassion, and the support of those who love you, you have everything you need to face each day and thrive.

You know that feeling when you're trapped in a storm, and all you want is for the rain to stop?

Hang in there, my friend, because storms don't last forever. Soon enough, the clouds will part, and the sun will shine on your face, warming your heart with its gentle rays.

LIFE IS A JOURNEY

We often get caught up in comparing
our journey to others...

...but let me remind you: your path is unique, and
it's meant for you. Embrace the detours, the
twists, and the turns, because they're shaping you
into the incredible person you're becoming.

Imagine life as a canvas waiting to be painted.

You hold the brush, and you get to choose
the colours that will shape your world. Embrace
the vibrant hues of joy, love, and gratitude,
and let your masterpiece reflect
the beautiful soul that you are.

LIFE IS A JOURNEY 

Life can sometimes feel like a roller coaster ride, with its ups and downs.

But here's the thing: even on the scariest drops, there's always a moment of relief, a breath of fresh air, and a glimmer of hope that reminds you to hold on tight because better days are ahead.

LIFE IS A JOURNEY

Picture this: you're standing in front of a mirror, and all you see are flaws and imperfections.

But guess what? Those perceived flaws are what make you unique and beautiful. Embrace your quirks, love yourself fiercely, and don't let anyone tell you otherwise.

We all have those days when our minds are swirling with negative thoughts, and it feels impossible to escape.

But let me tell you a secret: you have the power to challenge those thoughts, to replace them with positive affirmations, and to reframe your mindset. You're stronger than you think.

Life is like a puzzle, and sometimes
the pieces just don't seem to fit.

But here's the truth: you don't have to have all the
answers right now. Take it one piece at a time,
embrace the process, and trust that eventually,
the picture will come together beautifully.

You know those days when you wake up feeling like the weight of the world is on your shoulders?

Remember, it's okay to take things slow, to give yourself permission to rest, and to remind yourself that you're doing the best you can.

We all stumble and fall along the way,
but don't let those moments define you.

Embrace the lessons learned from your mistakes,
pick yourself up with grace, and keep moving
forward, knowing that resilience is woven
into the fabric of your being.

LIFE IS A JOURNEY 

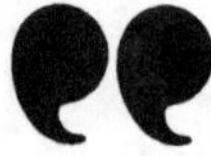

Life can be a wild adventure,
full of unexpected surprises.

When you find yourself facing an unknown path,
remember that it's an opportunity for growth,
for discovering hidden strengths, and for creating
beautiful stories that you'll share
with a smile one day.

LIFE IS A JOURNEY

SOUNDTRACK TO YOUR JOURNEY

Keep spreading laughter, my friend, and let it be the soundtrack to your journey through depression. With each giggle, chuckle, and belly laugh, you're reminding yourself that joy is always within reach. You're doing an incredible job, and I believe in you.

I have a feeling that the best chapters
of your life are yet to come.

You're like a book full of thrilling adventures,
hilarious plot twists, and heartwarming moments.

Can't wait to see what
the next page holds for you!

SOUNDTRACK TO YOUR JOURNEY 

Life is like a game, and depression is just a temporary level. But guess what?

You're leveling up with every challenge you overcome. Soon, you'll unlock the power-up that brings you to a whole new level of happiness.

SOUNDTRACK TO YOUR JOURNEY 

Depression may be tough, but you're tougher.

It's like a mosquito trying to bite a lion. Don't
worry, my friend, you've got the roar
and the swat to send it flying!

SOUNDTRACK TO YOUR JOURNEY 

You're not just surviving, you're thriving!

Each day you get up and face the world is
a victory. So, take a moment to pat yourself
on the back and give yourself a high-five
for being so incredible.

SOUNDTRACK TO YOUR JOURNEY

I have a feeling that your journey through depression will someday inspire others.

Your story is powerful, and it has the ability to touch hearts and bring hope to those who need it. Keep writing your incredible story!

SOUNDTRACK TO YOUR JOURNEY 

Depression may be a dark cloud, but you're the rainbow that breaks through, adding colour and beauty to the world.

Keep shining your vibrant hues, my friend. You bring so much brightness to those around you.

SOUNDTRACK TO YOUR JOURNEY

You're stronger than you think, my friend.

Depression may try to make you feel weak, but you have an inner strength that shines through. It's like a hidden superpower that gets stronger with every challenge you face.

SOUNDTRACK TO YOUR JOURNEY 

You're like a puzzle master, piecing together the fragments of your life with resilience and humour.

And let me tell you, the final picture is going to be absolutely amazing. Keep putting those puzzle pieces together, my friend.

SOUNDTRACK TO YOUR JOURNEY

Depression may try to make you believe that you're alone, but you've got an army of love and support behind you.

We're your cheerleaders, your backup dancers, and your comedic sidekicks. You'll never face this battle alone.

SOUNDTRACK TO YOUR JOURNEY

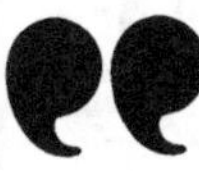

I have a feeling that happiness is your secret
admirer, just waiting for the perfect moment
to sweep you off your feet.

So, keep that smile on your face and
be ready for a grand romantic gesture
from joy itself!

SOUNDTRACK TO YOUR JOURNEY 

YOU'RE NOT ALONE

Listen, my friend, you're not alone in this journey. Reach out to those who care about you, seek professional help if needed, and believe that better days are ahead. Keep going, and know that you have the strength within you to overcome depression and embrace a fulfilling life.

Hey, I know it's hard, but try not to beat yourself up for having bad days.

We all have them, and it doesn't make you any less amazing. Be gentle with yourself, offer yourself kindness, and remember that tomorrow is a new chance to start fresh.

YOU'RE NOT ALONE 

You know what? Life can be tough, and
it's okay to feel overwhelmed sometimes.

Just remember that you're not alone in this.
Reach out to your support system, lean on them,
and let them remind you of your strength
when you forget it yourself.

I want you to know that it's okay to prioritise
your own well-being.

Self-care isn't selfish; it's a vital part of navigating
through the ups and downs of life. So, go ahead
and indulge in those small moments of joy and
relaxation that help replenish your soul.

YOU'RE NOT ALONE

You are so much stronger than you realize. I've seen you face obstacles head–on, and each time, you've come out even more resilient.

Believe in yourself, my friend, because I know you have the inner strength to overcome anything life throws your way.

You know, life is like a book, and right now,
you might be going through
a challenging chapter.

But let me assure you, my friend,
this is not the end of your story.

There are still countless pages waiting to be
written, filled with love, joy, and incredible
moments that will leave you in awe.

YOU'RE NOT ALONE 

It's natural to compare ourselves to others,
but trust me when I say that
you are enough just as you are.

You have your own unique talents, strengths,
and beauty. Embrace your individuality,
and know that you bring something special
to the world.

YOU'RE NOT ALONE

I want you to know that your feelings are valid,
no matter what anyone else says. You don't have
to justify your emotions to anyone.

Take the time you need to process, to heal,
and to find your inner peace. Your journey is
unique, and it's okay to take it at your own pace.

YOU'RE NOT ALONE

You're doing amazing, even on the days when it
feels like you're just going through the motions.
Your resilience shines through,
even in the smallest steps you take.

Celebrate those victories, no matter how small,
because they're all part of your journey towards
healing and growth.

YOU'RE NOT ALONE

You're not defined by your mistakes or setbacks.
They're just detours on the road to success.

So, embrace the lessons they bring, pick yourself
up with renewed determination, and keep moving
forward. Your resilience and ability to learn from
adversity will guide you to brighter days.

YOU'RE NOT ALONE

I want to remind you that it's okay to ask for help. You don't have to go through this alone.

Reach out to someone you trust, whether it's a friend, family member, or a professional. Opening up and sharing your burdens can bring immense relief and support.

RISE ABOVE DEPRESSION

You can conquer fears and rise above depression. Embrace laughter, courage, and a positive outlook. You have the power within you to face anything that comes your way. Together, we'll turn those dark clouds into rays of sunshine and fill your life with joy.

Hey there, depression! Guess what?

We're about to kick you out of our mind and throw a party for laughter and joy instead. Consider this your official eviction notice!

RISE ABOVE DEPRESSION

RISE ABOVE DEPRESSION 

You know what we're gonna do to fear?

We're gonna tickle it until it can't take it anymore!
Laughter is the secret weapon that'll help them
face their fears with a big smile on their face.

RISE ABOVE DEPRESSION

Depression,
it's time for a major makeover!

We're redecorating our mind
with bright colours, funny posters, and
an army of laughter. Say goodbye
to those gloomy days!

RISE ABOVE DEPRESSION

Fear, get ready to be bombarded
with laughter and positivity.

We're turning up the comedy volume
so high that you won't stand a chance.
Prepare to be disarmed by giggles!

RISE ABOVE DEPRESSION 

Depression,
we're turning the tables on you!

Brace yourself for a full-on humour offensive,
armed with jokes, puns, and hilarious moments.
Get ready to be overpowered by laughter!

RISE ABOVE DEPRESSION 

Brace yourself, fear, because we're planning a laughter flash mob in our mind.

When they least expect it, laughter will erupt, drowning out any negativity you try to bring.

Depression,
we're throwing a laughter party,
and you're not on the guest list.

Get ready for a night filled with giggles,
chuckles, and belly laughs. You won't be able
to resist the infectious joy!

RISE ABOVE DEPRESSION

Depression,
get ready for a major revolution!

We're launching a comedy coup, and happiness is about to take over. Say goodbye to those dark clouds and hello to laughter-filled days!

RISE ABOVE DEPRESSION 

We're gonna take fear by surprise and photobomb it with laughter and happiness.

Say cheese, fear, because we're capturing moments of pure joy that'll outshine any gloom.

RISE ABOVE DEPRESSION

A TRUE WARRIOR

You're a true warrior, my friend, and I have no doubt that you will conquer this. So, take a deep breath, gather your courage, and step out into the world with a heart full of bravery. Embrace the unknown, for amazing things await you just beyond the horizon.

Hey there, my friend! I want you to know that you have what it takes to overcome depression and come out on the other side stronger than ever.

You're a winner, and it's time to unleash your bravery and step out of your comfort zone.

A TRUE WARRIOR 

I know it can be scary to face the unknown,
but trust me, the magic happens outside
of that comfort zone.

It's like stepping into a whole new world
of possibilities and discovering
the incredible person you truly are.

A TRUE WARRIOR 

You've got this, my friend! Take a deep breath,
summon your inner courage,
and take that first step.

It might feel like a leap of faith, but you'll soon
realize that you have wings to soar to new heights.

A TRUE WARRIOR 

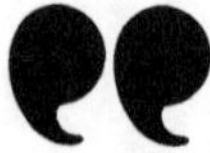

Remember, every journey begins
with a single step.

Start small, start with something that challenges
you just a little bit, and watch as you grow
stronger with each brave action you take.

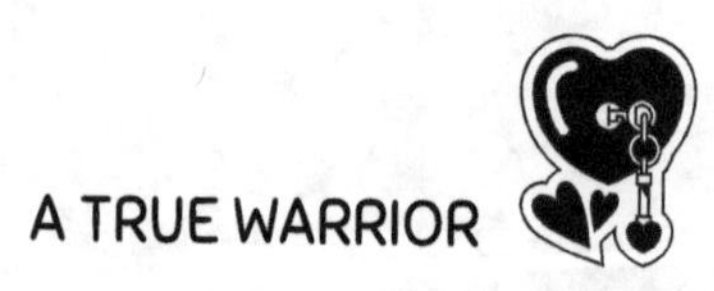

It's okay to stumble along the way, my friend.
Mistakes are part of the learning process,
and they don't define you.

Dust yourself off, laugh it off if you can,
and keep pushing forward. You're stronger
than any setback.

A TRUE WARRIOR 

Break free from the chains of self-doubt, my friend. Believe in yourself and your ability to conquer any obstacle that stands in your way.

You have the power within you to overcome this, and I have no doubt that you will.

A TRUE WARRIOR 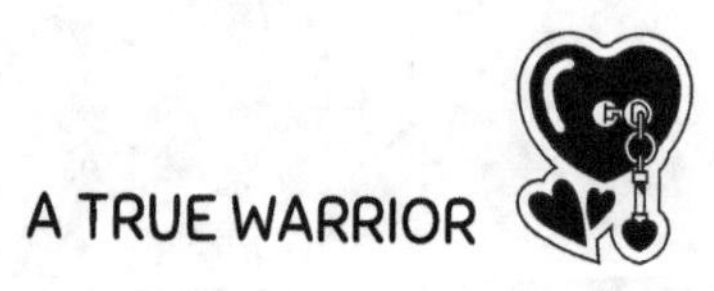

Surround yourself with people who lift you up, who inspire you to be your best self. Seek support from loved ones, friends, or even support groups.

Their encouragement will fuel your bravery and remind you that you're never alone on this journey.

A TRUE WARRIOR 

And hey, don't forget to celebrate your victories along the way. Each step forward, no matter how small, is a cause for celebration.

Treat yourself, indulge in something you love, and pat yourself on the back for being so incredibly brave.

A TRUE WARRIOR 

Take a moment to visualize your life beyond
depression. Picture yourself living a life filled with
joy, passion, and fulfillment.

Hold onto that vision, my friend,
and let it propel you forward.

A TRUE WARRIOR 

Remember, the world needs your unique gifts
and talents. Don't be afraid to share them
with the world.

Step into your own brilliance, embrace your
strengths, and let them shine brightly
for all to see.

A TRUE WARRIOR

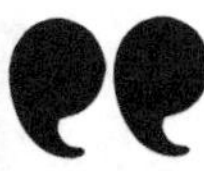

You're not alone in this, my friend. Reach out for help when you need it.

There are professionals, therapists, and support networks that can provide guidance and support along your journey.

A TRUE WARRIOR 

Above all, be patient and kind to yourself. Healing takes time, and every small step you take counts.

Believe in yourself, believe in your ability to rise above depression, and know that you are capable of creating a life that's filled with joy and happiness.

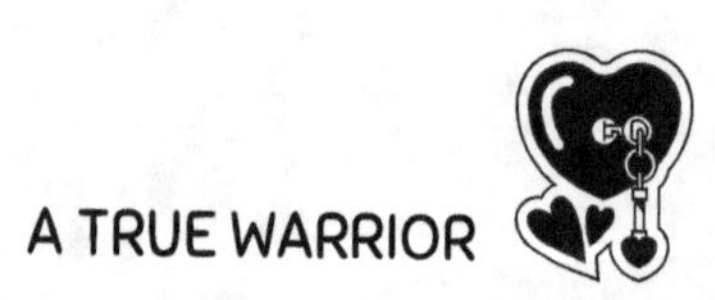

A TRUE WARRIOR

A LETTER FOR YOU

My dear friend,

I wanted to take a moment to reach out and remind you of how truly incredible you are. Life may feel challenging right now, and the weight of depression may be heavy on your shoulders, but I want you to know that you are not alone in this journey. I am here for you, cheering you on every step of the way.

Depression can make it difficult to see your own worth and the amazing qualities that make you unique. But let me tell you, my friend, you are a shining star in this world. Your kindness, compassion, and resilience inspire those around you. Your smile has the power to brighten even the darkest of days.

I know it's not easy to face each day when depression is clouding your mind and heart. But please remember that you are stronger than you realize. You have overcome countless obstacles before, and you have the strength within you to overcome this as well. Keep fighting, keep pushing forward, because I believe in you.

In those moments when darkness seems overwhelming, I encourage you to seek the glimmers of light. They may be small at first, but they are there, waiting to be discovered. It could be the warmth of a cup of tea, the sound of laughter, or the beauty of nature. Hold onto those moments, my friend, and let them be a reminder that joy and happiness still exist in this world.

Remember to be kind to yourself throughout this journey. Treat yourself with the same love and compassion that you extend to others. Take time for self-care, engage in activities that bring you joy, and surround yourself with people who uplift and support you. You deserve all the love and care in the world.

While it may feel like the weight of depression will never lift, I want you to hold onto hope. Hope is a powerful force that can guide us through the darkest of times. It may flicker, but it never truly fades. Believe in the possibility of a brighter future, my friend, because it exists for you.

You have so much strength within you, and I believe in your ability to overcome this chapter of your life.

Keep holding on, keep being brave, and remember that brighter days are ahead.

You are loved, you are cherished, and you are deserving of all the happiness in the world.

THANK YOU

Dear Reader,

I wanted to take a moment to express my heartfelt gratitude for your decision to purchase this book.

Thank you for placing your trust in me and for embarking on this journey of healing and self-discovery.

I want you to know that you've made an incredible investment in yourself.

By picking up this book, you've shown a willingness to confront the challenges of depression head-on and to seek out the tools and knowledge needed to navigate this journey.

I truly hope that the words within these pages provide you with comfort, inspiration, and practical guidance as you navigate the ups and downs of your own unique path.

While I can't promise an instant cure for depression, I can promise that this book is filled with effective approaches to help you along your path to healing.

Remember, my friend, this journey is not about perfection. It's about progress. Every step you take, no matter how small, brings you closer to a life filled with joy, meaning, and purpose. So, be gentle with yourself and celebrate each milestone.

But please remember that this is just a starting point. You have the power to adapt and personalize these strategies to fit your unique needs and circumstances.

Throughout this book, I aim to provide you with not only practical advice but also a sense of hope and encouragement.

It's my sincerest wish that you find comfort in knowing that you're not alone. There are countless individuals who have walked a similar path and emerged on the other side, stronger and more resilient.

If at any point you find yourself feeling overwhelmed or in need of additional support, don't hesitate to reach out to your loved ones, a trusted therapist, or support groups.

Remember, seeking help is a sign of strength, and there is no shame in asking for support when you need it.

Once again, I want to express my deepest gratitude for choosing this book.

Together, let's embark on this journey with an open heart, an open mind, and a shared commitment to reclaiming your happiness and well-being. You are not alone, my friend, and brighter days are within reach.